IMAGES OF ENGLAND

ELLAND

IMAGES OF ENGLAND

ELLAND

BRIAN HARGREAVES

TEMPUS

Frontispiece: Southgate runs centrally through this aerial photograph. Mass demolition of Elland town centre in the 1960s saw the demise of many ancient thoroughfares. Casson Place, Radcliffe Fold, Post Office Yard and others disappeared from the map. Redeveloped Westgate runs along the bottom of this photograph. Boxhall Road has not yet been made. Huddersfield Road runs nearly parallel with Southgate enclosing the new blocks of flats.

First published 2005

Tempus Publishing Limited
The Mill, Brimscombe Port,
Stroud, Gloucestershire, GL5 2QG
www.tempus-publishing.com

British Library Cataloguing in Publication Data.
A catalogue record for this book is available from the British Library.

ISBN 0 7524 3703 8

Typesetting and origination by Tempus Publishing Limited.
Printed in Great Britain.

Contents

Acknowledgements

In preparing the material for this book I received help and information from many sources. Most of the photographs are from my own collection but I would like to thank the Greater Elland Historical Society, the Calderdale Library Service, Margaret Hanner for her help with the material on Cooper Kitchen, Margaret Mitchell for the information she supplied for the Elland at Play section, Donald Haigh and Richard Garnett for their help with information on St Mary's choir and Michael Bailey for his help with information on the Bailey family. My thanks also go to Albert Rinder for his very informative introduction.

I also greatly appreciate the help given by David Hargreaves in editing, sometimes brutally, and typing the text and Emily Hargreaves for her assistance and interest, also to my wife Margaret for her patience and proofing of the text.

Brian Hargreaves
2005

Introduction

In AD 80 the Roman general Agricola defeated the local tribe of Brigantes at Castle Hill, Almondbury and later a road was built on the hillside south of Elland and a fort constructed at Slack. This camp was abandoned in around AD 125 and another road built over Blackstone Edge. A road was later constructed along the north side of Elland, a camp was established and this was called Carbodunum. A Roman altar was found at this site and the inscription on it reveals the date AD 208. When the Romans left Britain, in AD 410, the Anglo-Saxons began to inhabit the area, which was called Ea-land. 'Ea' represented water and 'land' a building. The Domesday Book of 1086 records that Gamel, of Ealand, owned three and a half carucates for geld, a pasturable wood and four acres of meadow.

Leising de Eland, in around 1150, was granted a coat of arms described in Hopkinson's Manuscripts as, Barry of five, gules and argent, six Martlets–Orle three, two, one. Leising built Elland Hall at the north side of the River Calder and several generations of his family lived there. His son, Henry, was responsible for the building of St Mary's church in Elland. The most renowned member of the Eland family was Sir John de Eland who, in 1317, was granted a Royal Charter that allowed him to hold a weekly market and two fairs annually. The year 1341 saw the start of the 'Elland Feud' with the families of Quarmby, Lockwood and Beaumont of Crossland Hall. In 1354 members of these families murdered Sir Thomas de Eland and his son John, leaving no heirs to the de Eland family in Elland. Isobel, the granddaughter of Sir John de Eland, inherited the estate and later married Sir John Savile of Tankersley.

After the Elland Feud two branches of the Savile family lived in the Elland area. Sir John Savile lived at Elland Hall. After his death, his second son, Henry, who had married the heiress Elizabeth of Thornhill, inherited the Savile Estates. During the Civil War, Sir William Savile served under Lord Newcastle. In 1648, Lord Fairfax with 700 men, laid siege to Thornhill Hall, but they met with strong resistance from Lady Anne Savile. However, after six days, Fairfax allowed Lady Anne to leave with her son George and they went to Rufford Abbey. Later George married Mary, the daughter of George Talbot and Bess of Hardwicke and he became the owner of the Elland Estates. George Savile was a notable politician in the reigns of Charles II, James II and William III and during this time he received many honours including that of the Marquis of Halifax.

Another branch of the Saviles came into the Elland area with marriages to the heiresses of Rishworth and Copley. Thomas Savile lived at Hullen Edge and his descendants were benefactors of St Mary's church until the death of their last member in 1608. Nicholas, the fourth son of Thomas rebuilt New Hall in the late fifteenth century. The Saviles of New Hall played a prominent part in the life of Elland and, in 1610, John Savile rebuilt part of the hall including a rose window of six mouchettes over the main entrance. In the main hall is a very large plaster coat of arms of Charles II. Henry, the third son of John Savile obtained land in Bradley and his son John rebuilt Bradley Hall in 1577. John became a famous judge and Baron of the Exchequer. The second son, Henry, became Warden of Merton College, Oxford and was responsible for the translation into English of parts of the authorised version of the Bible in 1619. These Saviles lived at Methley and later became the Earls of Mexborough.

Christopher Saxton made the earliest map of Elland, the area near Park Wood, and in 1614 his son, Robert, mapped out the Hullen Edge area. John Ogilbie constructed road maps from York to Chester, via Leeds and Elland. He also made a route from London to Scotland, which passed over the River Calder at Elland. Celia Fiennes on her journey from Rochdale to Leeds bypassed Halifax and described Elland in glowing terms in 1698. In 1745, General Oglethorpe, on his march from Wakefield to Manchester, passed through Elland and his wife rested in the area we now know as the junction of Westgate, Long Wall, and Hullen Edge Road. Lady Oglethorpe was enthralled by the spectre of three roads above each other, Bank Bottom, Long Wall and Overgate. When the troopers rested for the lady to admire the view, George Readyhough sold them some of his home-brewed ale, or 'galker'. This delay, it is said, resulted in the column of soldiers being too late to apprehend Bonnie Prince Charlie, who had made his escape back to Scotland. In 1750, William Mann produced *A plan of Ealand with the Town Fields and Crofts*. Henry Power of New Hall became a well-known physician and another famous doctor was John Crowther, who discovered a method of preventing gangrene in compound fractures.

In 1855, Robert Dempster became the manager of the Elland-cum-Greetland Gas Company and also established the Rosemount Ironworks in Huddersfield Road. The firm produced gasholders and had the largest workforce in the area. The introduction of North Sea gas later lead to the firm's closure. Other industries to figure in the economic stability of Elland have included coal mining and quarrying for the making of Elland flags and brick making. Joseph Dobson founded the confectionary firm of Dobson's in 1850, now the oldest surviving family business in Elland. Thomas John Dobson introduced the famous 'Yorkshire Mixtures'.

For centuries textiles were the main industry in Elland. In the Poll Tax returns of 1371 there is an entry for Hugh Stephenson, Alice and Isabel of The Cross, websters (weavers). From 1790 to 1803, New Street was built and most of its inhabitants made woollen cloth for Thomas Casson, who later built large factories including Norton Mills on Savile Road. The Canker Dyke that flows from the Ainley hillside provided water for many mills including Spa Well and Marshall Hall Mills. The river and canal also provided water for many mills including the Smithies Mill with its water wheel. There were also many mills within the town itself. Working hours and conditions were arduous. In 1962, there were over sixty businesses working within the textile trade in Elland - today there are no textile mills at all.

In 1663, the southwest entrance gate to St Mary's church housed a school. In that year there is an account for three shillings for its repair. In 1911, the school amalgamated with the girls' grammar school to become Elland Secondary School, later Elland Grammar School and now the Brooksbank Sports College in Victoria Road. In 1718, Frances Thornhill founded a school in Elland as did Grace Ramsden in 1734. The National School, renamed the Church of England School, was opened in 1846 in Westgate.

Between 1850 and 1866, many improvements were made to St Mary's church, described by the *Halifax Guardian* as becoming one of the most beautiful and interesting churches in Yorkshire. The non-conformists increased in number and a dissenting house was built in Westgate in 1691. In 1756 a Presbyterian church was built at the bottom of Langdale Street. James Ashworth established the Baptist chapel in Jepson Lane. In 1789, James Cartledge persuaded the minister there to take over at Blackley Baptist church.

After visits from John Wesley, a chapel was built at the top of Eastgate which became known as the Dog Lane Chapel. Another chapel was built at the lower end of what is now Coronation Street and known as Central Hall. In 1914, St Paul's Methodist church was erected at South End. In 1824, the Methodist New Connexion built Bethesda Chapel at the junction of Victoria Road and Jepson Lane. In 1866, a Sunday school was built and in 1880 the old chapel was pulled down and a new chapel built. The Sunday school became unsafe and was pulled down but the front entrance is now preserved.

Elland has also played a part in social or sporting activities. In 1828, Elland Music Society was formed and by 1846 they were giving concerts with various instrument players and singers. Sporting activities included the game of knur and spell, played originally in a field behind Jepson Lane. Elland Cricket Club moved to their new field at Hullen Edge in 1876 and two years later they played host to the visiting Australians.

A host of stories can be told about Elland people. One such tale is of the pinder who had the pinfold opposite the town hall at South End, behind the prison. Business was very slack and so one day he went up towards the Ainleys where he saw a cow and calf standing at the gate. He looked around, and seeing no one, he opened the gate and drove the cattle towards the pinfold. The good lady of the house had seen this occurrence and joined the procession. When they reached the pinfold, the pinder had to go in front to open the gate. The lady gave a piercing whistle; the cow and calf pricked up their ears, turned around and followed the lady back to their field. My name, by the way, is Rinder, not Pinder!

Albert Rinder
2005

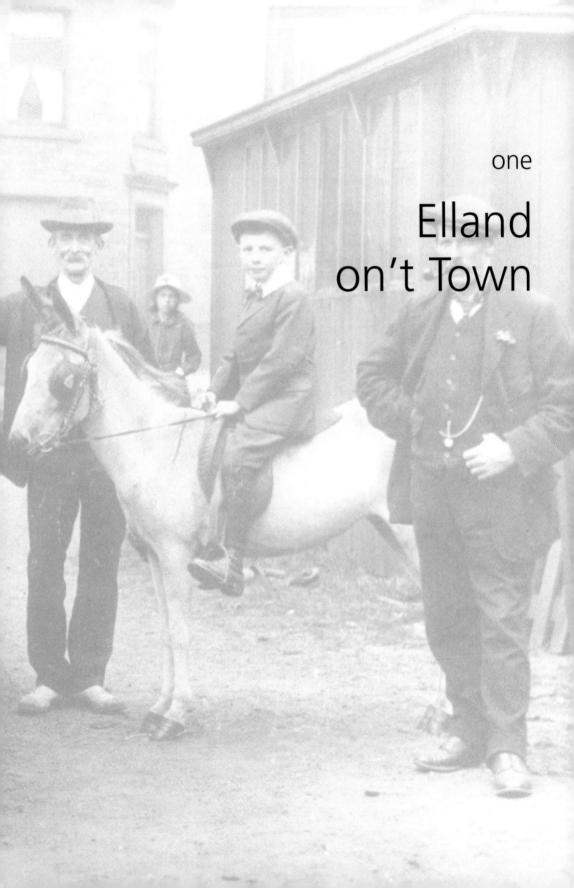

one

Elland on't Town

There was a stone cross beside the Savile Arms Hotel in 1850. Before St Mary's church was built it is thought that a preaching cross was situated in this area and itinerant priests gathered people there for prayers. The crowd awaits the arrival of an Elland Carnival procession at The Cross during the Edwardian era. The man situated centrally is holding an 'anti -vibration Elland bicycle'. The Savile Arms, built in 1748, is on the left.

Opposite above: London House, ladies and gentleman's outfitter is just visible on the far left and Thomas Bros beers, wines and spirits is seen in the centre. Manchester House is to the right. Members of the Forrest family ran this draper's shop for many years. Lloyds Bank, far right, eventually moved into Southgate and moved again to its present position at the junction of Southgate and Coronation Street in November 1990.

Opposite below: The row of shops at The Cross was drastically altered in 1910. The top section was removed from Manchester House and the premises between there and the bank on the corner of Northgate were made into two shops.

Looking towards The Cross, the Savile Arms Hotel can be seen behind the clock. The shop on the left offers the service of re-covering umbrellas. At the far end of the run of buildings on the right, a shoemaker advertises his wares.

Opposite: From early in the century until the 1950s many towns had a Maypole Store, purveyors of dairy goods. The Elland Maypole was at 27 Southgate and here the smartly dressed staff pose for the photographer.

Elland post office before it was moved to its present site in July 1910. This building was situated on Southgate, nearly opposite what is now the Yorkshire Bank. The young boy, second left, is James Brearley, who later became well known as an auctioneer in Elland. The Conservative Rooms doorway had a staircase leading to the upper rooms, which were later an accountant's offices.

Opposite above: A busy scene in Southgate. The postal worker is standing by the Blue Barrel. The Royal George is across the street and the Wellington Inn is to be seen in the background.

Opposite below: A similar view but quieter scene. The Post Office Chambers are on the left. The Royal George, on the right, closed in 1912. The sign above the horse and cart is advertising W. Wadsworth Teeth.

Southgate
Elland 58

Southgate, Elland.

Opposite: The Health Food Stores had moved from Westgate because of demolition and was later to move into Victoria Road when the same fate befell this part of Southgate. After closure as a public house in 1912, the Royal George had many uses as shops and storerooms.

Left: Southgate, seen here in 1947, is eerily deserted, although the shadows indicate that it is early in the day. The building on the immediate left is the Liverpool Stores, which until 1910 was Elland's main post office. The corner doorway is the entrance to the Blue Barrel Inn, 31 Southgate, built in 1830. It survived until the mass redevelopment of the 1960s and was closed on 2 January 1965 when Maurice Schofield was the licensee.

Below: Milton Smith had a pie shop immediately facing into Portland Street. The Blue Barrel Inn is on the right at the junction with Southgate. This inn had a room that was frequented by mill owners and businessmen. It was known as the 'House of Lords'.

This scene from around 1900 is of Southgate looking towards The Cross. Repair work is being carried out on the building at the bottom of Kiln Lane, now Coronation Street. Advertisements abound: look for Rowntree's Chocolate, Colman's Mustard, Dr Lovelace's Soap, Sprat's Dog Food and many others. The Yorkshire Cricket Council poster tells us of matches between Elland and Castleford, Halifax and Hull. Admission to the ground at Hullen Edge was 3d and ladies were admitted free. The building under repair survived to become a butcher's shop and next-door, to the left, later became the shoe repair business of the Horsfall family. The row of shops to the right and those immediately opposite survived until the 1960s.

Opposite above: The dominant building here was a farmhouse situated at the bottom of what is now Coronation Street. Alan Kitson, a local milkman, occupied it until its demolition in 1901. The sign on this building advertises a cricket match between Halifax and Elland.

Opposite below: Southgate from the bottom of Kiln Lane, which became Coronation Street on the accession to the throne of King Edward VII. Rabbits can be seen hanging outside the shop on the right. Iredale's is next-door across the passage.

Advertisements abound in this view of Southgate. The Liverpool Store was situated in the Post Office Chambers. The Bass sign hangs outside the Blue Barrel and the Brooke Bond Tea sign is very prominent. The shop second from the right is the Penny Bazaar, which seemed to sell everything. It was run by the Brook sisters until it closed due to redevelopment.

The hardware store of Cooper Kitchen at the time of this photograph was at the junction of Southgate and Coronation Street. Cooper Kitchen continues to trade from the central part of this row of shops and Lloyds Bank now occupies the corner site. The detached building in the middle distance is Field House. The lower portion of this building was redeveloped to house retail units.

The dairyman poses in front of Field House, *c.* 1904. This house was for many years the residence of Drs Holton, Foster and others. Behind this building, in Crown Yard, a painted sign denotes the entrance to the Surgery.

A quiet view of Southgate. The men on the right-hand side of the road are underneath the sign of the Wellington Inn, which is advertising Bentley and Shaw Beers. Immediately across the road is the shop of Cooper Kitchen. In the foreground, the sign of A. Smith invites us to purchase blouses and lingerie. Redevelopment of this building in 1924 removed the frontage to realign it with the neighbouring shops. On the right is the butcher's shop of C. Rhon.

Joseph Dobson founded a confectionary business in 1850. Dobson's specialised in 'Bridal Cake and Funeral Biscuits'. They began to concentrate on boiled sweets and by 1900 the confectionery business was discontinued. Sweets are still manufactured at their Northgate factory and the business continues to trade to the public from these premises.

Opposite above: The 1920s and transport is predominant in this view of Southgate taken from the junction with Victoria Road. The milk float with its flat-capped attendant waits outside the post office that still has a corner doorway. The vehicle parked outside Cooper Kitchen is a substantial motorcar and is in sharp contrast to the sleek vehicles of today. The sign on the wire support pole reminds us to Beware of the Cars. The tramcars ran very close to this corner. Frank Heap's chemist shop, to the left, is advertising Iodised Throat Lozenges at 8d and 1/3d.

Opposite below: The dilapidated building here is South House. Before this site was a centre for local government it was a family house. It had a large, walled garden which extended over Elizabeth Street and part of what is now the Town Hall Square and Marketplace. South House was demolished and the building that is still known by many as the Council Office was erected. Members of the newly formed Elland Urban District Council, met at the new offices on 4 January 1895. This arrangement for council meetings allowed the town hall building to be used for other purposes. The sign of the hanging boot is outside what was Freeman, Hardy and Willis and the shop with the awning is now an opticians.

Work begins on the foundations of Victoria Swimming Baths. The contract for this work and also the building of Turnpike Street was given to Rhodes & Co. of Bradford. This company became insolvent and another contractor completed the work. The swimming baths opened on 22 November 1902.

This photograph gives us a lost view of the fire brigade station, the ambulance carriage house and a nursing room and, on the first floor, a chemical laboratory. The newly erected Council Offices are visible on the extreme left.

A view of Victoria Road from Southgate with soldiers marching away to the horrors of the First World War, many not to return. The building to the left, with the stone gateway, is Lowfield House, which was occupied in 1906 by Dr A. Morton. It is now a dental surgery.

This gathering in the Town Hall Square in 1916 seems to be the equivalent of our modern car boot sale. Items are being offered for sale and all receipts converted into relief parcels for local men fighting in France and elsewhere during the First World War.

A throng of people gathered in Elland Town Hall Square to celebrate the Armistice of November 1918. Some people have found a viewpoint on the roof of the Victoria Swimming Baths. The property behind and to the right is part of the Town Hall Buildings.

Town Hall Square looking towards the junction with Victoria Road. Tramlines and wires are visible on the Elland to West Vale route. The buildings on the left now house a dental practice, a solicitors' office and a Chinese restaurant.

The Town Hall, though never used as such, dominates the junction between Southgate and Huddersfield Road. It was built in 1887 on land given by Sir John Savile. The building had a clock tower but no clock until 1909 when Lewis Mackerell presented one in memory of his father James Mackerell, former Chairman of the Elland Urban District Council.

Opposite: An invitation to the starting of the new Town Hall clock on the 8 June 1909. This invitation was to Mr H. Mackerell and lady.

Programme of Proceedings.

3–0 P.M.

Starting of New Clock by Mrs. Mackrell.

Mr. Clarkson will ask Mr. Lewis Mackrell to present the Clock.

Mr. Mackrell will formally present the Clock and hand over the Title Deed to the Chairman of the Council.

Acceptance of the gift by Mr. Hyde Sharratt, J.P., Chairman of the Council on behalf of the town.

Mr. J. F. Crossland, Chairman of the Directors, will also acknowledge the presentation on behalf of the Town Hall Company.

Supported by Ald. Smithies, J.P. and County Councillor Peel.

3–30 TO 5 P.M.

Music and light Refreshments.

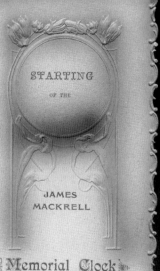

STARTING

OF THE

JAMES
MACKRELL

Memorial Clock

JUNE 8th, 1909.

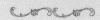

Fern Place,
Elland,
4th June, 1909.

Mr. Lewis Mackrell requests the
pleasure of the Company of

Mr. *H. Mackrell*

and lady at the Town Hall,
Elland, on Tuesday, June 8th at
2·45 p.m., on the occasion of the
presentation of a Clock to the
town in memory of his father.

[OVER

Huddersfield Road runs virtually parallel to Southgate. In the centre background is Cocker's Mill, which later became Ely Garnett and Sons Ltd. The towers of the Wesleyan Chapel, which opened on 4 October 1892, can be seen on the skyline and the Temperance Street Methodist church, now the Cartwheel Club, is on the right.

Three children pose for the photographer close to the junction of Southgate, Catherine Street and Huddersfield Road. St Paul's church has not yet been built and there is no town hall clock, which dates this scene to before 1909. The young boy is Sidney Mitchell, eventual keeper of Mitchell's Cash Stores close to this spot. Herbert Mitchell founded the shop in 1892.

The little girl stands on Yorkshire setts, as she gazes through the mist towards Huddersfield, where Catherine Street meets Southgate and Huddersfield Road. In the background stands Mitchell's Cash Stores, which on closure was purchased by a locally renowned firm of jewellers and horologists to extend their premises.

Before 1821, the town stocks and lock up were situated near to the parish church. Elland Gaol, at South End, was subsequently built and during its time was used as a police station, a secondary school for girls, a lending library, a meeting room and a bus shelter. Over the main door can be seen the emblem of the West Riding Constabulary and a stone bearing the inscription 'Who so keepeth the law is wise'. This stone is now set over the door of the Social Service offices in Elizabeth Street. The dilapidated stocks are nearby.

A side view of Elland Gaol, showing the staircase leading to the upstairs room. This was for some time used as a gentlemen's meeting room known as 'The Pinfold Parliament'. The posters announce many events, including a public lecture by J. Howard-Reed on 'Japan, The Land of the Rising Sun'. This was to be held at the Constitutional Hall on Wednesday 23 November 1904. The building on the left is part of South End School, which was opened on 7 January 1878.

Opposite above: The Town Hall, St Paul's church and the Salvation Army Citadel, in this 1930s view of Huddersfield Road. A very ornate telephone box can be seen adjacent to the steps of the Town Hall. A pair of mangles stand at the entrance to Dick Taylor's yard before a row of wooden shops. The gable end of the gaol can be seen just beyond these.

Opposite below: Dick Taylor sits on his cart in his breakers yard behind R.G. Murduck's photographers shop in Huddersfield Road. Dick Taylor was born in 1878 and died in 1936. The boy on the pony is Dick's son William. George Ray, standing on the extreme right, worked for Elland Urban District Council.

ELLAND—HUDDERSFIELD ROAD.   10027

Traffic of a much steadier pace than today's negotiate 'the Ainleys', Huddersfield Road, in the late nineteenth century. The horses and carts are likely to be servicing Sharratt's Brickworks, just visible through the mist and steam, halfway up the hill.

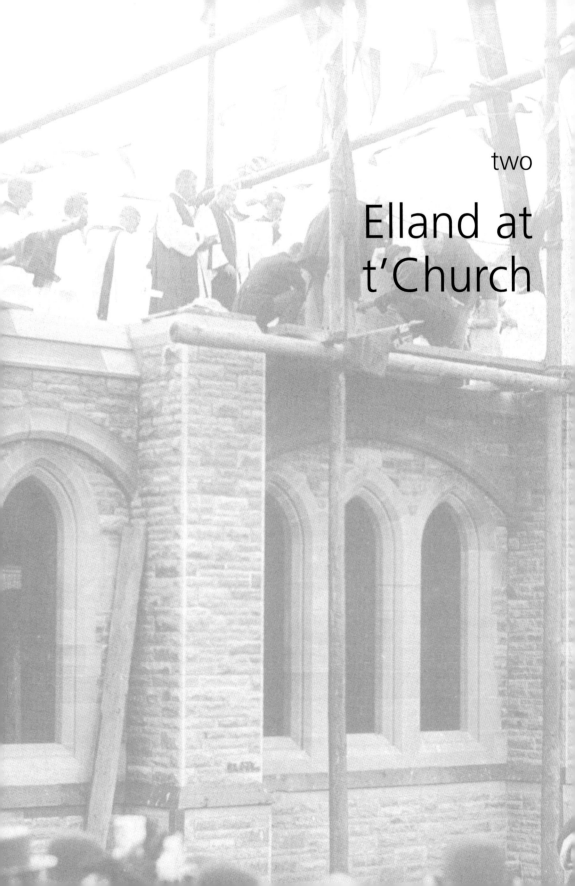

two

Elland at t'Church

A Congregational church choir outing, early in the twentieth century. On the front row left, kneeling and wearing a trilby hat, is Albert Townsend, the well-known Elland photographer. Standing on the right in the back row is Fred Carter, who kept a boot and shoe shop in Victoria Road. Sitting on the wall in the centre is Herbert Spencer, who worked at the Albert Mills of Joseph Smithies at Bank Bottom. When new boys started working at the mill he painted their clogs red to denote they were learners.

Opposite above: Three days before Christmas in 1894 a mighty storm wrecked the Baptist church at Upper Edge. It had been opened only three and a half years earlier and built at a cost of £3,000. An organ was added only eight months prior to the gale. The sides and roof of the building collapsed and the pews and pulpit were crushed. The church was not insured against storm damage and it cost £1,450 to rebuild.

Opposite below: This view of St Thomas's church at Greetland is from a postcard dated 10 April 1909 and includes a group of girls, three of whom are wearing 'Ascot' style hats.

This card, postmarked 5 May 1914, is addressed to the Revd R. Wilson, St Margaret's Rectory, Durham. The message includes '…this is a snapshot of our church' and is signed 'T.I.J.'. St John's church, West Vale, was opened in 1880 and closed just short of its centenary year. Latterly it was converted to offices.

The young people of Middle Dean Street chapel, West Vale, line up to take part in the Elland Carnival procession of 1970. The wagon is gaily decorated and has white-walled tyres. The slogan on the cab door says, 'Ingham's Yarns weave best – try them and test'. George Ingham was at Prospect Mill, West Vale.

Building began on St Paul's Methodist church in 1914 and it was completed in 1915. It was built after wooden shops were removed from this busy junction of Catherine Street and Southgate. It has a fine tower and steeple but no bells. It is now known as Southgate Methodist church.

St. Paul's Elland 28th Halifax Scouts,
1927.

The man in this view is standing on Jepson Lane outside the Parish Rooms. This was the first Baptist chapel in Elland and it was built in 1772. After losing its minister to Blackley, the building was used by various groups including the religious sect known as the 'Thumpers, Ranters and Secularists'. In 1895 the owners, the Ashworth family, gave the building to the parish church for use as a parish hall. When the hall was demolished to allow Jepson Lane to be widened and straightened a replacement building was required and this was the Parochial Hall in Westgate, which was opened on 27 April 1929. The gable ends of the ancient Fleece Inn can be seen over the high enclosing wall, part of which was removed in 1966.

Opposite above: Cubs, Scouts, Rover Scouts and Scout Leaders pose with their bugles, drums and a large shield outside St Paul's church in 1927. This was the 28th Halifax Scout Group.

Opposite below: This finely decorated wagon, full of young girls, prepares to join a procession in Stainland during the Edwardian era. The Providence Congregational church supported the Band of Hope.

'Top o't street Chapel' was built in 1824 at the junction of Townfield Lane, now Victoria Road and a very muddy and stony Jepson Lane. In 1863 the Minister, the Revd T. Addyan, lived in one of the two cottages and the caretaker lived in the other. On 28 March 1878 the occupiers of the two cottages were given notice to quit. The following year the chapel was demolished and the area cleared by 3 May 1879. On the same day six stones were laid to commemorate the building of a new church, Bethesda.

This aspect of Bethesda Church and schoolroom is no longer available. The schoolroom was built in 1866 and enlarged to a two-storey building in 1878. It was demolished in 1999/2000 and this opened up a long lost view of the front of Bethesda Church, which was completed in 1880. The grassed area in the foreground is at the junction of Savile Road and Victoria Road.

Lucy Hammerton was born in 1824 and was a lifelong member of St Mary's church. She served in many capacities including that of Sunday school teacher, along with her sister Emma. The sisters lived for many years at Hammerton House, Westgate, which was built by their uncle Ernest Hammerton. In support of Canon Winter's appeal for funds to build All Saints church, Lucy wrote a book, *Olde Ellande*. This book gives a fascinating glimpse of life in Elland during the nineteenth century. The area in Westgate known as Hammerton Close is near to where Hammerton House was sited and is named after the Hammerton family.

All Saints church is built on land given by Lord Savile on Savile Road. During the 1890s, with congregations increasing, it was felt that Elland needed another church in addition to the parish church of St Mary the Virgin. This was the scene on 11 August 1901 when Lord Savile laid the foundation stone of All Saints church.

Opposite above: It was always difficult raising the money to pay for the new church. On a number of occasions work had to be suspended until further funds became available. Public appeals were mounted and the building was opened for services on 4 November 1903.

Opposite below: Money was again the problem in 1906 when the church had debts of £2,182. All Saints was consecrated on 12 July 1912. In 1913 an anonymous gift of £7,000 allowed the church to be completed and the building of a Sunday school. The church has a copper-plated steeple, or fleche, which is surmounted by a gold painted figure of the Archangel Gabriel.

Local stone was used to build All Saints church. Red brick with stone dressing is featured inside the church and there are many statues of Saints at the chancel arch and also on the reredos of the altar.

A group of young people from All Saints church enjoy an outing into the Yorkshire Dales at Whitsuntide in 1931. The woman fifth from the left in the front row is Olga Finan. She later married Charles Dyson who for many years ran a shoe repair business in Victoria Road.

Opposite: The church of St Mary the Virgin was founded in 1180 when stonemasons came to Elland after completing Kirkstall Abbey. The early church was of a simple design, probably an aisle-less nave and chancel, which has been added to over the centuries. The tower was erected in around 1490. The gentleman at the church gate is Mr Harry Johnson who was verger/caretaker at St Mary's. He lived at Dundyvan, next door to Wainwright Hall and his daughter Gertrude Johnson was headmistress at the Church of England School. Mr E.W. Crossley, who attended the church, owned the coach and Broad Lea Mills, Dewsbury Road.

Left: Canon Ernest Winter arrived in Elland in 1893 as parish priest. He quickly decided that another church was required in the town and became the driving force behind the fundraising and building of All Saint's church. The canon preached his last sermon on Sunday 14 January 1917 at St Mary's. He collapsed on leaving the pulpit and was carried to the vestry where he died.

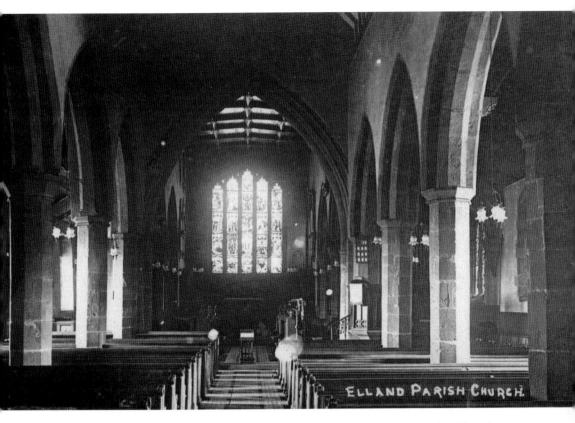

A pre-1914 interior view of St Mary's, affording a view of the magnificent east window. Alterations during the Victorian era resulted in the dismantling of the gallery which was supported by the pillars on either side of the nave.

Opposite below: The edifice of St Mary's church dominates this view. The Norman bell-cote, one of only seven remaining in England, can be clearly seen in its place above the chancel arch. The renowned east window was completed in the fifteenth century but was severely damaged by Commonwealth troops who were billeted in Elland during the Civil War. The graveyard was significantly reduced to accommodate the making of Huddersfield Road, shown in the foreground. Graves were moved and bones stored in the bonehouse below the east window. On the right, Grace Ramsden's school is visible. In her will, drawn up in December 1734, she made provision for the founding of a school for poor boys in the township of Elland-cum-Greetland. The first school of 1741 was on the site of the present building. The school closed in 1966 after which it was used by Elland St John's Ambulance Brigade and Red Cross Society. It is now a children's nursery.

The east window, the chancel arch and the rood screen are all seen in this interior view of St Mary's. The rood screen, figures, and altar rails were erected by public subscription in memory of Canon Winter and were dedicated in 1920. In a recent refurbishment the rood screen was moved to the west end of the church. The font was moved to its original position beside the chancel arch and portraits of Moses and Aaron have been restored and placed on the north and south walls. The seated minister is the Revd Bernard Pawley.

The Elland St Mary's church Lads' Brigade gathers in 1928 for a group photograph. The bass drummer is Arnold 'Dick' Taylor who was for many years the caretaker at the West Vale mills of John Horsfall. Seated fourth from left in the front row is Ronnie Walton who worked for British Rail in Huddersfield.

Ministers, officials, choir and friends at St Mary's in the early 1950s. The ministers are, to the right, Revd Bernard Pawley and Curate Michael Pumphrey. Seated next to Revd Pawley is Ernest Haigh who was the organist at All Saints church from 1912 until 1941 and then at St Mary's. His son Donald, seated next to Michael Pumphrey, is currently organist at the church having succeeded his father. Fifth from the right in the front row is Alan Chesters who was to become Bishop of Blackburn. With their church wardens' wands are, fourth from right, Miles Prestwich and fourth from the left, Joseph Garnett.

This view of the south face of the clock tower of St Mary's dates to the celebration of the Silver Jubilee of King George V in 1935, when many public buildings were floodlit. The original single clock face was replaced in 1911 with an illuminated four-faced mechanism. The graveyard on the south side of the church is known as 'the Lord's side' housing the bodies of 'righteous people'. The graveyard on the north side of the church is known as 'the Devil's side' housing the bodies of murderers, suicide cases and allegedly unbaptised children.

three

Elland at
Work

Joe Bailey came to Elland in the late 1840s. He worked for the Halifax Co-operative Society where he later became manager. Joe and his family lived in Westgate and there he opened a small shop, next to the house, where he sold homemade cakes and bread. Joe died on 5 August 1893 at the age of sixty-two and is buried at Elland cemetery. His wife Susannah lived until she was ninety-five and died on 21 March 1926.

Albert Bailey, son of Joe, was born 1855. As a young man Isaac Dewhirst, a local worsted spinner, offered him an apprenticeship at his mill. Albert married Emma Park on 15 April 1879 and they set up house at 63 Westgate and there he opened a grocery business, following his father into the trade. Albert and Emma had nine children and all were born in Westgate.

Right: An advertising leaflet for the Bailey shops.

Below: Albert's first shop in Westgate. The entrance to New Street is in the foreground and Albert Street, built by Albert Bailey and grandly named after himself, is the next street on the left. The railings on the right are of Hammerton House, *c.* 1962. After almost 100 years of business, and a change of ownership to Mr and Mrs Lister, the shop finally ceased trading and was demolished in 1969.

A. Bailey & Sons,

Family Grocers
and Provision
- Merchants -

BAILEY'S for COFFEE
BAILEY'S for T E A S
BAILEY'S for DANISH BUTTER
BAILEY'S for BACON

90, SOUTHGATE
Telephone 104
and
- 63, WESTGATE -
Telephone 104A

- - ELLAND - -

Albert's second shop was at No.90 Southgate. The window on the right is in Elizabeth Street and the staff are seen here very smartly turned out in white smocks and aprons. Today a Chinese restaurant occupies this building.

Albert Bailey rented Riverside Mill in 1910 and renewed his interest in worsted spinning. This view of Riverside House, the mill house, shows Emma Bailey, on the left, with her daughter Annie that same year. Shortly afterwards the house was demolished to make way for more factory space.

Four generations of the Bailey family pose at Riverside House. Albert is on the left, Ernest, his son, is on the right. Susannah, his mother, is seated holding baby Margaret.

An example of early stationery used at Riverside Mill before 1945. The spinning company was named Albert Bailey & Sons Ltd to differentiate it from his grocery business just known as 'A. Bailey'.

Albert Bailey, in the centre, stands in the yard of Riverside Mill in the mid-1920s. Albert continued as chairman of the company until his death in 1930.

Many mills organised trips to the seaside or pantomimes and Bailey's was no exception. Here, an outing of the late 1950s shows, kneeling, left to right: Beryl Clark, Rita Clark, -?-, Audrey Barker. Standing,: -?-, Brian Hopkinson, Peter Flather, Norris Fletcher, Emily Whip, Ronnie Williamson, -?-, Rose Williamson, Audrey Williamson, Alan Temple, Audrey Armitage, Edith Proberts, May Lamb, Dorothy Sutcliffe, Elaine Mallinson, Eleanor Proberts, Ethel Caldwell, Doris Fox.

This view of Riverside Mill is dated before 1910 and Riverside House can be seen on the left. A bypass for Elland was proposed in 1963, the route of which was expected to affect Riverside Mill. A public enquiry held in 1969/70 overruled all objections and the scheme was given the go-ahead. A compulsory purchase order was served on the company in February 1975 and a notice of closure to the employees the following May. Production ceased in September of 1975 and the mill was vacated by February 1976.

The building at 44 Southgate is easily recognisable but the surrounding area has changed dramatically. Cooper Kitchen who arrived in Elland from London built Moorgate Chambers in 1872. The building jutting out into Southgate, with the 'Blakey's Boot Protectors' sign, was demolished and the building line brought back to Moorgate Chambers in a rebuilding programme of 1898/99. On the right can be seen one of the two narrow lanes that ran from Southgate to Victoria Road, before Coronation Street was made.

Cooper Kitchen was an engineer and he manufactured tricycles, double tricycles and bicycles at his London works and also at the Moorgate works in Elland. Owing to illness, Cooper Kitchen was confined to a wheelchair for the last twenty-seven years of his life and he began trading in hardware when the cycle business ceased manufacturing.

An example of Cooper Kitchen's Elland 'Anti-Vibration Bicycle' now housed in a Glasgow museum.

The founder of the business died in 1926 but the ironmongery and hardware shop continued as Cooper Kitchen Ltd. All these aluminium pots and pans make a grand window display here in the 1930s.

The bottom of Coronation Street can be seen here with one corner of Central Hall (built 1855) housing the Radio Relay shop. Garden tools, wringing machines and stepladders are among items displayed outside Cooper Kitchen in the 1950s.

Moorgate Chambers is seen in all its glory in this image from the 1960s. The original building of 1872 and the later addition of 1898-99 can be seen, with the join in the two buildings visible.

Electricity was first generated from Lowfields in 1903 when the burning of the town's rubbish was used to raise steam to drive the generators. The scheme did not pay and an auxiliary station was opened in Timber Street. In 1949 the first mention of a new station for Elland was put down on paper. On 5 August 1955 the site at Lowfields had been prepared for building to commence.

Opposite above: On 7 August 1959 the power station was generating electricity and connected to the National Grid. The station had three 60-megawatt generating units. The ash settling ponds can be seen in the middle distance. The ash was the residue from the coal that was burned in the mighty boilers. The official opening of the station took place on 28 April 1961 and was performed by Mr A.R. Cooper, a member of the Central Electricity Generating Board.

Opposite below: To allow for the increase in volume and weight of traffic on the approach road to Lowfields and the power station site, Wistons Lane had to be widened and resurfaced. This photograph, taken on 10 September 1954, shows a steamroller preparing to roll down the lower layers of road after the machine behind has stripped off the upper layers. The building on the right is part of the Nu-Swift complex.

By 4 October 1954 significant progress had been made in the state of Wistons Lane. The small sign above the dumper truck directs us to Albert Bailey's Riverside Mill, seen at the extreme right. The gasholders behind belonged originally to the Elland-cum-Greetland Gas Company, which was founded in 1836.

Opposite above: A steam locomotive makes its way towards Brighouse on 14 March 1957. The fields behind are now filled with houses on the Grasmere and Thirlmere estates and with Old Earth School. Lower Edge Road is to be seen at the top of the picture.

Opposite below: Coal was delivered to Lowfields by road and rail. This Hudswell 'Elland No.1' shunting engine served for many years at Elland and on station closure was bought by railway enthusiasts for preservation.

Opposite above: Shortly after 2.00 a.m. on 22 November 1971, fire raged through the coal conveyor used for transporting fuel to the bunkers situated in the top of the boilerhouse. The conveyor was completely destroyed.

Opposite below: On 24 November 1971 mobile cranes were introduced to support and help dismantle the fire-damaged conveyor. By 1 December a temporary conveyor had been erected on scaffolding.

Left: This handbill was issued to announce an open weekend at the power station to celebrate twenty-five years of generation at Lowfields. Technical data on the station includes: years generated: 1959-1991; coal used: 13,000,000 tons; availability: 90%; staff: 160 (at full strength); thermal efficiency: 29.95%.

Below: The power station viewed from Ainley Top on 2 October 1984. The redbrick houses in the middle distance form the Elland Lane estate and Caldercroft housing development has yet to be built on the land in the foreground. The station closed in 1991 and the site was cleared to make way for Lowfields Industrial Estate.

Left: The weir at Elland Bridge in March 1963 with Elland Power Station and the gasworks beyond. The weir was breached and damaged beyond repair by a storm in 1966.

Below: The mighty Elland Mills straddled the River Calder on the downstream side of Elland Bridge. A diverted section of the river was originally used to drive water wheels. A fire was discovered shortly after 7.00 p.m. on 31 October 1904. It quickly spread and the mill was soon engulfed. At this time the mill was occupied by a cloth fuller on the ground floor and by cotton doublers on the other floors. Evidence of this building has now almost completely disappeared.

Providence Mill in Elizabeth Street is busy on 16 September 1927. This mill suffered a disastrous fire in 1942. The land is now occupied by Flower Acre. The clock tower of the Town Hall Buildings can be seen at the right.

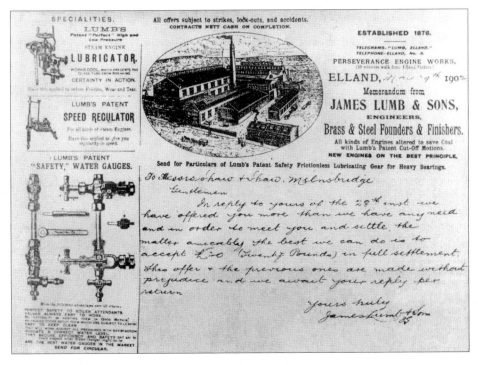

The Perseverence Engine Works of James Lumb & Sons in Dewsbury Road was founded in 1876. It was advertised in 1902 as being 'ten minutes walk from Elland Station'. This letter dated 29 May 1902 is regarding settlement of an outstanding debt.

Emily Whiteley stands by her pair of looms in the weaving shed of 1916. Health and Safety officials of the modern day would frown upon her long skirt and the unguarded cogged wheels.

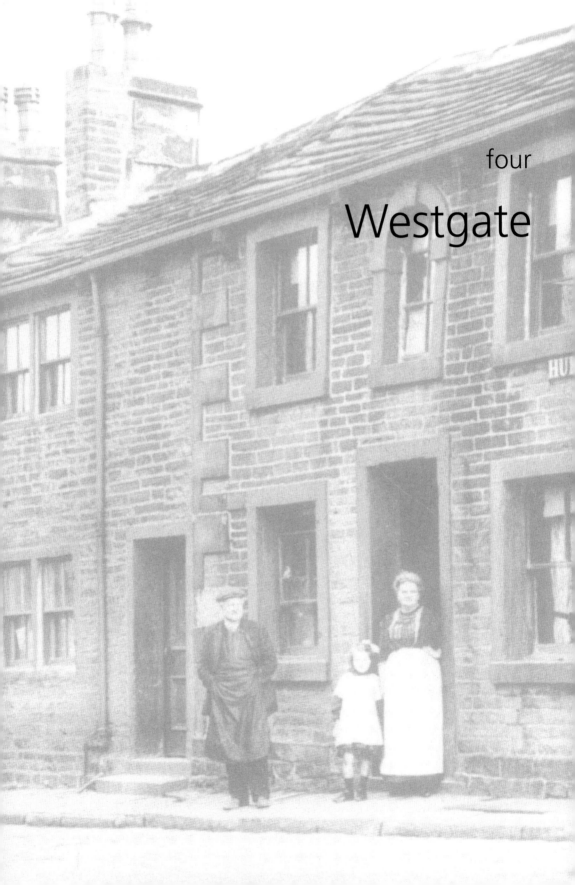

four

Westgate

The postman and his customers stand before houses that were soon to be demolished to make way for the tramway, which was extended from Elland to West Vale in 1914. The road disappearing centrally was known in ancient time as Overgate and is now Hullen Edge Road. Between the cottages on the right and the houses beyond is the entrance to Long Wall, which was the main route from Elland to Rochdale.

These cottages are on the left in the previous photograph. The lady standing in the doorway is Mrs Thornton, who was reluctant to move to allow for demolition but eventually bowed to the inevitable. A large retaining wall was built from the stone released by the demolition. The arched window above Mrs Thornton's front door was built into this wall and can still be seen at the foot of Hullen Edge Road.

The view from Park Avenue in 1974. Hullen Edge Road is in the foreground, with Jepson Lane sweeping in from the right towards Long Wall. Westgate is in the cente and the white car is parked outside the 'Little Shop' which had been an early Elland fire station. At this time Ken and Jean Fletcher were the proprietors. These properties were demolished soon after this picture was taken. The block of flats known as Towngate House had yet to be built.

These children look to be in their Sunday best in the early 1900s. This is Westgate near to the entrance of the Ellen Royd estate, now the clinic. The owner of this property was Joseph Smithies who also owned Albert Mills in Bank Bottom (Saddleworth Road). The houses on the extreme left are without roof tiles and are in Gog Hill. They were thought to be of the Stuart period.

Wooler's shoe shop stands on the corner of New Street and Westgate, with Squire's furniture store next door. The detached building below is Gledhill's the printers. The railings of the National School are to be seen further down Westgate.

The railings border the playground of the Church of England school, formerly the National School, which was rebuilt after a fire in 1942. The property across Westgate illustrates how narrow the road was. All of these shops and houses, including Regents Place in the centre of the picture, were swept away in the wholesale demolition of the early 1960s.

It is difficult to ascribe sex to the children seated on the doorstep, as it was common at this time for boys up to a certain age to be in dress-style garments. Lower down the street the Benefit Boot Stores have their wares hanging outside.

The sign indicates that Caroline Brier was the landlady of the Mexborough Arms and Swale's shop looked well stocked when this photograph was taken in the early years of the twentieth century. Window cleaners are busy at Thomas's wine and spirits shop. The gates of St Mary's church can be seen at the top of Church Street.

Looking up Westgate the bills are posted on the gable end of the Saville Arms. In 1906 the house with the shutters was that of Tom Turner Brook, chemist and tax collector. Number 5 was the grocery store of Thomas Swale. The Mexborough Arms was at No.7, and was formally known as The Talbot. It closed on 24 December 1927. The building opposite, under the sign with the gable, was the Barley Mow. It closed on 20 October 1898, when Samson Haigh was the occupier.

NEW INN

ERNEST MARSDEN.

ALE, PORTER, SPIRIT
LIQUORS and TOBA

NOTED

STONE TROUGH ALES

five

Elland at t'Pub

The Fleece Inn is the oldest public house in Elland and after the parish church is the oldest building in the town, dating from 1603. It was originally a farm building known as the Great House. Ale has been brewed at this location for centuries and as we have heard already there is a story about ale being served from here to troopers making their way to Manchester to apprehend Bonnie Prince Charlie in 1746.

> *'Be warned ye thoughtless - ne'er that place frequent,*
> *Where precious time's in sinful pleasure spent;*
> *Where sinners meet and revel all the night*
> *And mix in riot, drunkenness and fight;*
> *Frequent it not, nor its bad company know,*
> *For there lo! I received a fatal blow'.*

This epitaph appears on the gravestone of a man allegedly murdered at the Fleece Inn. William Wooler, proprietor of the inn at the time, stated in his diary that the incumbent of St Mary's church, the Revd Christopher Atkinson, had told a parishioner that Wooler kept a disgraceful hostelry. The parson made sure that everybody knew this by adding the rhyming inscription to the man's tombstone. Wooler was organist and choirmaster at this time and the disagreement between him and the Reverend was long and acrimonious.

John Edward Briggs stands in the Fleece Inn yard to the right of the doorway, which has the date 1610 carved into the lintel. After many alterations, this doorway is now inside the building. John E. Briggs was known as 'Merry Legs' and married the daughter of the landlord of The Wheatsheaf, which was nicknamed the 'Three Bonnie Lasses', a reference to the licensee's daughters. It closed on the 28 December 1935 when Frederick Henry Wade was licensee.

Above: This bar in the Fleece Inn was known as the kitchen and until the late 1960s it had a sign on its door stating 'Gentlemen only'. When refurbishment took place in 1974 the range was removed and an inglenook fireplace was revealed, the outline of which can be seen. The round-backed chair was the subject of much mystery. It was claimed that it had been seen to 'dance' without assistance!

Left: The Fleece Inn was a very popular meeting place and many organisations used its facilities. Musicians and singers performed oratorios on a regular basis. One infamous visitor was Joachim von Ribbentrop who came here when he was working as a wine salesman in the early 1920s. He later became Adolf Hitler's foreign ambassador and was hanged following the Nuremberg trials in 1946.

Licencees of The Fleece Inn

1806	- 1823	J. Pollard
1823	- 1845	W. Wooler
1845	- 1855	J. Thornton
1855	- 1871	M. Thornton
1871	- 1895	M. Stansfield
1895	- 1897	M. Etherington
1897	- 1903	J. E. Briggs
1903	- 1939	B. Garside
1939	- 1949	H. A. Exley
1949	- 1965	E. Bentham
1965	- 1967	J. J. Wood
1967	- 1970	M. Boyd
1970	- 1975	J. Clarkson
1975	- 1977	G. Bradley
1977	- 1979	M. Forrest
1979	- 1982	D. Ainsworth
1982	- 1984	M. Le Vay
1984	- 1985	J. H. Hardaker
1985	- 1985	L. Haycock
1985	- 1993	K.A. Wheatcroft
1993	- 1993	M. J. Bull
1993	- 1993	M. Corrigan
1993	- 1995	S. Buxton
1995	- 1996	M. Jones
1996	- 1997	G. M. Smith

Left: The Fleece has had some notable licensees since 1806. We are indebted to William Wooler for leaving us his diary, which gives an insight into life at the Fleece Inn and the surrounding area. Mary Thornton has a son, Samuel, who was headmaster at the National School in Westgate. Graham Smith was the last licensee before a name change from the Fleece Inn to the Great House in 1997 referencing the building's original name. In 2004, Neil Monkman became the first licensee of the Fleece Inn's second creation.

Below: The Fleece Inn building today stands alone, but years ago it was part of a complex of houses, workshops, barns and all manner of farm buildings. The major Fleece Inn barn was also the home of the mysterious 'Leatherty Coit'. At midnight, so it is said, the large barn doors would open without assistance and out would dash a coach pulled by headless horses, driven by a headless coachman who was Leatherty Coit. The coach would make for Old Earth and then return to the barn. This spectre created a sudden rush of wind and when people heard it they would say, 'There goes Leatherty Coit'.

Above: Northgate, sometimes referred to as Well Hill, on a sunny day in 1908. The two men stand outside Nutton's decorators shop. The Rose and Crown public house is seen centrally and bears the date 1689 over its doorway. It was built as a town house as opposed to a farmhouse or a manorial building. Robert Tiffany was the licensee when the closed on 19 December 1914. The shop on the right was Jowett's men's hairdressers and it was later the Elland office of the *Halifax Courier.* The girl second from the left is Evelyn May Ingham. She married Herbert Ingham who had a furniture shop at the junction of Southgate and Boxhall.

Two houses with a central passage way were drastically altered to make the Star Inn in New Street. It sold Bentley's famous Yorkshire beers and it was a 'beer-only house' until very late in its existence. New Street had a number of public houses including: the Fox and Grapes, the Hanging Gate, Bird In Hand, Gardeners Arms and the Cherry Tree Inn, which was kept, at its closure by 'Auld Bellywark'.

The Wellington Inn is an older building than the name suggests. There is some evidence that it is a timber-framed building of the mid-seventeenth century. The inn is mentioned in the census of 1881 as being occupied by Ben Bottomley and his wife Delia. They later moved to the Bird In Hand in New Street. A butcher's shop is attached to the inn in this drawing. Lancelot Bowes ran it for a period in the mid-nineteenth century.

Opposite, below: A busy scene on Park Road, *c.* 1895. The Station Hotel, now The Barge and Barrel, stands to the left. As in most towns and cities it was common to find a substantial hotel near to the railway station. An advertisement appeared in the *Halifax Guardian* on the 10 January 1880 inviting brewers to bid for a 999-year lease to erect a building to be known as The Railway Hotel. This name was never used. On the 30 January 1880 a bid of £45 per year ground rent was received from Joseph Wilson and this was the successful bid.

George Frederick Barrowclough had his name over the door when this trip was organised in the mid-1950s. Back row, left to right: George Bowler, Joe Blackford, Jack Smith, Nellie Blackford, Kenneth Falkingham, Roy Stancliffe, Muriel Smith, George Barrowlough (licensee), Jack Robson, Jennie Barrowclough, Gordon Hill, Mick Fatherly, Harold Robson, Eddie Robson, John McConnel. Seated: Irene McConnel, Mrs Fox, Jessie Robson, Mrs Smith, Mrs Astin.

Opposite above: In 1890 James Morton was licensee of the Barley Mow in Westgate. The *Brighouse Echo* of 30 September 1898 reported that an application to renew the licence by Mellor Shepherd was refused because 'the house was of a disorderly character'. An appeal was lodged before Wakefield Quarter Sessions, to be held on 17 October 1898 and the Barley Mow was allowed to remain open while the appeal was being heard. It closed on the 20 October 1898 having lost the appeal. Samson Haigh was the licensee.

Opposite below: The Spring Gardens was built in 1810. In 1838, Samuel Webster acquired a small brewery and supplied free houses. He bought his first public house in 1845. Webster's took over the Shibden brewery of Joseph Stocks, which had supplied the Spring Gardens at 45 Elland Lane. Fred Stafford was the licensee in 1903.

During the reign of the first Queen Elizabeth, a number of new inns were built and later many adopted the name New Inn. The New Inn, at No.5 Briggate was of a much later vintage. Wooler records that Mrs Chambers left the New Inn on 4 November 1840. The Inn closed on 30 April 1956.

Two sets of isolated stone steps suggest an already demolished building at the junction of Jepson Lane and Westgate. The staircase with the handrail leads to a working men's reading room known as the Snake's Nest. Hanson & Son of 32 Southgate, Halifax took advantage of a gable end to advertise their furniture sale. The Snake's Nest was demolished before 1914.

The Horse and Jockey Inn was situated beside Ainley Woods. The rise in popularity of horse racing and the allied gambling it produced resulted in a number of public houses adopting associated names. It is recorded that Elland Racecourse was laid out between Townfield Lane (on Victoria Road) and South Lane. One of the last meetings was in 1790. The Horse and Jockey closed on 27 December 1933 when Lily Louise Daltry was the landlady.

Joseph Henry Brook was licensee of the Horse and Jockey Inn, leaving in 1926 to live in the new red-bricked houses of Park Avenue. Joseph had three daughters, the eldest being Emma who later kept the Penny Bazaar and became a local councillor. Joseph Brook is seen here, in a white shirt, seated on the front row to the extreme right.

The Bird In Hand was located at 23 New Street. It was a fully licensed house. When Thomas Casson built the George and Dragon, now the Old Bailey in Huddersfield Road, the licence was transferred from the Bird In Hand. Dan Marsden took out a beer-only licence and changed the name to the Foresters Arms. It later reverted to the original name. Moses Freeman was the landlord when it closed on 23 December 1908.

The cottage beside the Royal Hotel was in 1855 the Crown and Anchor Inn. It was demolished to make way for the building of the Halifax and Huddersfield Union Bank, which opened in 1895. This area listed a number of public houses including: the Jolly Boatman, the Staff of Life and the Live and Let Live. The Royal Hotel, now the Bridge, and the Malt Shovel are still trading.

The Golden Fleece, Blackley. The smart tackle on this horse and the junior jockey obviously impressed the judges at an Elland Carnival of the 1920s as this entry took third prize. Fred Carter stands with his arms folded beside Mrs Carter. In September 1898 an application was made to incorporate a one-roomed cottage into the public house. The police objected to the application on the grounds that such an increase was unnecessary in so small a village. The application was granted.

The Tavern in Stainland Road, West Vale, closed on the 18 April 1959 and John Doyle was the landlord. Other public houses to close include: the Clothiers Arms at Brow Bridge, which closed in December 1926 and the Prince of Wales in Stainland Road, which closed on New Year's Eve 1937. Mrs Ward was the landlady at the Bridge Hotel, Rochdale Road when the doors finally closed on 10 August 1967.

Left: Julia Crowther stands with a waiter and a customer by the front door of the Rising Sun Inn, Jepson Lane, before 1914. The inn was originally two cottages, occupied by the minister and caretaker of the Jepson Lane Baptist chapel. One bricked up doorway can clearly be seen. The inn was demolished and a new Rising Sun rose further back to allow the road to be straightened and widened to accommodate the new tramway, which opened on 29 May 1914.

Below: This building that was the Bath Tavern was in Ainley Road, now Huddersfield Road. In common with a number of beer houses it was also a working farm and got its name from a reference to the healing powers of the waters from the Canker Dyke which ran nearby. The made up arched doorway next to the outbuilding was the entrance to the tavern.

six

West Vale

The first recorded mention of Clay House is in 1419 when Robert Clay was in residence here. The eastern gables were build in around 1630 and the western gables were completed before 1700. The Clay family ceased ownership of the house in 1693 upon the death of John Clay.

The Public Hall, West Vale with St John's church in the centre and the school on the left. The Public Hall was formerly the Mechanics' Hall and church services were held there on Sunday evenings from April 1879 but it soon became evident that a church was required in West Vale. On Shrove Tuesday 1880 a tea and entertainment was arranged which made £30 profit, of which £18 was put towards building a new church. On 16 October 1880, Mr John Baldwin of Clay House laid the foundation stone of St John's church.

Herbert Fox ran the Victoria Music Rooms in Saddleworth Road. The window sign tells us 'Instruments delivered on receipt of first payment'. This building is now Greetland post office.

A drayman and children line up obligingly for a photographer in Saddleworth Road. The shop of Herbert Fox can be seen on the extreme right. This area is still known by many as 'The Adelaide', so named after the wife of King William IV.

WEST VALE—STAINLAND ROAD.

The tramway was extended to West Vale from Halifax in August 1905, terminating at the Shears Inn. The base for the chimney of North Dean Mill can be seen on the extreme left. The large building to the right of the tram is the Brig Royd Mill.

The No.7 tram has arrived at the West Vale terminus from Huddersfield. Passengers for Halifax had then to alight and walk into Stainland Road to catch a Halifax Corporation tram. There was no through route from Huddersfield to Halifax because of a difference in line gauges.

The corner property of John Eastwood's butchers shop is now the Shears Inn. Originally the inn was situated where the adjoining car park now stands. It was demolished in 1965. The cottages behind are in Bowers Yard. A section of tramway can be seen in the foreground, which dates this scene to sometime after 1905.

This tram has literally reached the end of the line on its journey from 'post office' to 'West Vale'. One of a chain of Economic Stores is on the right with Eastwood's butchers shop on the opposite corner. The lamp standard acts as a signpost pointing out Elland and Barkisland. The shop to the left of the tram is advertising Kay shoes and this sign is almost outside the Shears Inn which is set back from the road.

The hoist for unloading goods at the Economic Stores can be seen against the sky and further along Stainland Road we can see a barber's pole and umbrella sign. It was common at this time for barbers to repair 'gamps', parasols and the like. The white building is the Shears Inn. It was originally Lambert or Lambard House and is mentioned in deeds and documents dated August 1557. This tram has an enclosed upper deck and is advertising Websters Café in Halifax. The buildings on the left of Stainland Road are the Victoria Mills of J. Sutcliffe, now Andy Thornton's Architectural Antiques. The large Brig Royd Mill was demolished in 1973.

Locally these houses are regarded as the only houses in West Vale. As a postal area, West Vale does not exist and comes under the umbrella of Greetland. Contradictorily it seems that most of the people in this photograph are leaving the 'West Vale' mills of John Horsfall. The railway viaduct can be seen along Saddleworth Road and the signpost tells us that Halifax is to the right and Stainland to the left.

The Clay House Mills of Wright Hamer & Sons dominate this view of Brow Bridge. The cottages on the left include Jack's Fish Shop and just on the bend in the road is The Bridge Hotel.

The very heart of West Vale is the junction of the turnpike roads from Barkisland and Stainland constructed in 1825. In 1850 a tollhouse stood at this junction. On Wednesday 19 February 1851 plots of land were put up for sale in the almost empty fields adjacent to Lambert House (the Shears Inn). Lot 5, an area of 610 square yards, was land occupied for many years by Peel's chemists shop.

A fine body of firemen is seen here outside the Fire Engine House at West Vale. It was situated in Calder Street as part of the Public Hall. The Elland Brigade served West Vale, Greetland and Stainland in the early years, but it became increasingly obvious that the outlying areas required their own service. This engine was purchased from the Crossley Carpet works at Dean Clough, Halifax. The photograph is dated 1907.

seven

Elland at School

Brooksbank School, founded by Joseph Brooksbank in 1712. Joseph lived in London but was the son of John Brooksbank of Elland who died in 1702. The amalgamation of boys' and girls' schools resulted in the building of the present school in Victoria Road. It was opened in 1911 and this is a scene recorded shortly afterwards.

In 1894 a new school was built in Westgate and was known as the Grammar School. The school had two storeys with one large room on each floor. In later years this building was known as the Brooksbank Institute and was home to a number of organisations including the Elland detachment of the St John's Ambulance Brigade. It was demolished in 1965.

The National School in Westgate was opened in 1846. A commission of 1865 described it as 'an excellent school' and suggested the possibility of it being a 'middle class' school. Here a pony grazes on land now occupied by the Parochial Hall, which was opened in 1929. Local rhyme: 'Nash bogs. Dirty dogs. Can't afford to clean their clogs'.

In 1942 a disastrous fire ravaged the National School. This resulted in scholars being transferred to other local schools including South End, West Vale, Holywell Green and use was made of the Brooksbank Institute and temporary buildings in the adjacent Boxhall recreation ground.

During the Second World War people were encouraged to grow their own produce. The school in Westgate used land behind the Parochial Hall to this end. Boys of the school are seen 'Digging for Victory'. One of the school's air-raid shelters can be seen on the left.

Elland Church of England School (formerly the National School) - class photograph, 1966. Back row, left to right: David Crossley, Paul Austin, Andrew Roberts, Clyde Darson, Ian Sheard, Jonathon Magee, Adrian Mitchell, Glen Macarthur, Kenneth Bradbury, Miss Edith Gledhill. Middle row: Julie Roberts, Jill Williamson, Thelma Wimpenny, -?-, Richard Hanson, Ian Hill, Michael Hargreaves, Lesley Sykes, -?-. Front row: Lesley Greenwood, -?-, Judith Harrison, Susan Roberts, Julie Blackburn, Ann Gledhill, -?-, Janet Williamson, -?-, Dawn Squires.

South End School was opened on 7 January 1878. The land between the photographer and the school is now occupied by the Town Hall Buildings. The school was demolished in the mid-1980s to make way for a new supermarket. Stone and features of the school were incorporated into the new building.

A South End schoolmistress keeps a wary eye on her Class II girls in the late Victorian period. When the school closed, pupils were transferred to Cross Lane and Old Earth at Lower Edge.

In common with most Board schools West Vale had separate entrances for boys, girls and infants. It was opened in 1878 and was as a direct result of urban sprawl, which occurred, in the mid-Victorian age when the children of families working in the newly erected mills required school places. The crown-topped fountain was erected to commemorate the sixtieth year of the reign of Queen Victoria, by Alfred Speak of Ingwood and is dated November 1897.

Boys at West Vale School, *c.* 1912. Seated centrally in the sailor suit is Willie Ramsden, later Councillor Ramsden of Elland.

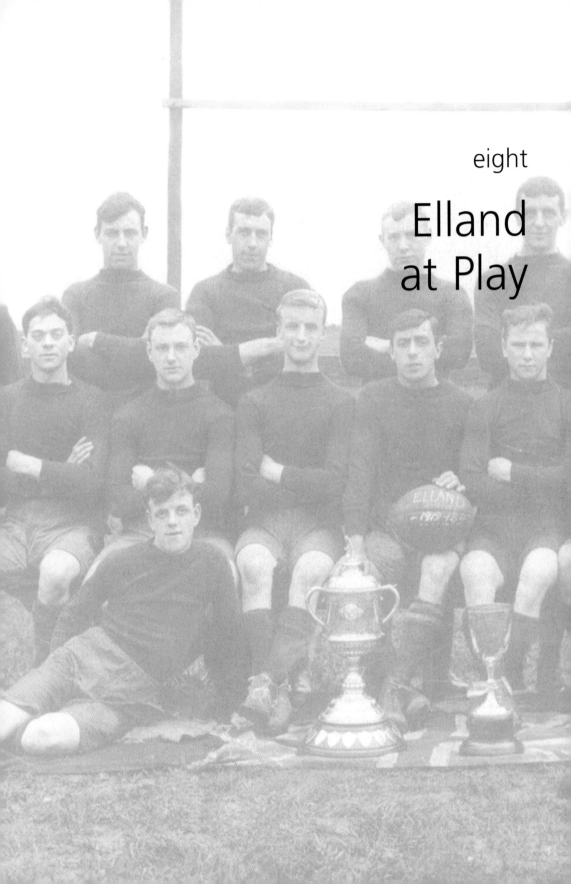

eight

Elland
at Play

The banner, accompanied by Elland Silver Band, tells us that this is Challenge Shield Final day. Looking from Victoria Road towards South End, the bottom of Elizabeth Street can be seen in the centre. The grocer's shop has not yet become Bailey's at No.90 Southgate and is still under the name of Littlewood. Thomas' bakery now occupies the middle building on the right.

Knur and Spell was a well-established game in the Victorian and Edwardian eras. The spell was suspended in a type of sling and the object was to hit this piece of wood, ivory or some other suitable material as far as possible with a carved stick – the knur. The man on the left is Eli John Sutcliffe and he and his companion are in a field at South End. Houses in Quebec Street can be seen behind Mr Sutcliffe.

Fred Sutcliffe was involved in all kinds of sporting activities in Elland throughout his life. Here, he is seen after winning the Sharrat Cup for swimming in 1913/14.

Here is a young Fred Sutcliffe, in shiny clogs, standing beside a magnificent Rugby League trophy. The approximate date is 1907.

Members of the Elland Primitives AFC pose with their medals after winning the league in 1914/15. The side aspect of the Zion Chapel is seen behind.

The ball carries the legend, 'Elland 1912-1913 Reserves'. This team won the Elland Rugby League Cup in that year. The man sitting at the far right is Stanley Brook.

Left: The Elland Football Club issued this In Memoriam card to honour Oliver Smith.

Below: Spectators at Elland Cricket Club. In 1860, teachers and pupils at Providence Independent Sunday school had the idea of forming a club. Matches were played in a field off Hullen Edge Road, not far from their present home. George Herbert Hirst began his illustrious career at Elland and Bill Bowes, another Yorkshire stalwart, was born in the town.

St John's church, West Vale, had a ladies cricket team and here in around 1890 the match is between ladies and officials. Men are fielding and can be seen wearing top hats. The mill chimney behind is the Prospect Mill of George Ingham. The match is being played in a field later occupied by Lumby's Engineering Works.

The 5th Halifax (Elland) Company of the Boys' Brigade and the 1st Elland Company of the Girls' Brigade formed the Anchormen Drum and Bugle Corps. The Anchormen fronted Elland Carnival procession annually for many years. They were highly successful in national competition; being Boys' Brigade Champions on a number of occasions and following disassociation from the Boys' Brigade were regularly in the top five of the National Drum Corps United Kingdom Championships. The anchor remained their emblem and a later uniform had tailed jackets and tricorn hats.

nine

The Bridge

Elland Hall started life as a thirteenth-century, timber-framed structure, one of the oldest in West Yorkshire. Building continued for a further 600 years but the hall became a victim to the building of the Elland bypass. It was carefully dismantled in the 1970s with a view to rebuilding it on another site but this notion has never materialised. An earlier road-widening scheme of the 1930s saw the demolition of the building on the left, which was Lily dyeworks. The single storey building on the right is the bridge tollhouse that disappeared in the late Victorian era.

Elland Hall still dominates the bridge. Lily dyeworks still stands although the tollhouse has gone. The earliest mention of a bridge over the River Calder at Elland was in 1199, when it was probably of a wooden construction. The area at the northern end of the bridge is shown on older maps as 'Woodbridge'.

At the southern end of Elland Bridge stand the Bridge and the Malt Shovel public houses. In this photograph, dated 1894, the Bridge was the Royal Hotel and the cottage next door was demolished. The Royal Hotel has a sign announcing Billiards and an 'Ordinary' which was a workman's lunch, served at 12.30. Note that the bridge has not yet been widened.

This card postmarked May 1903 is of a similar view to the previous photograph with some major changes. The Bridge has now been widened. It was reopened on 13 November 1897. A fine building, which started life as the Halifax and Huddersfield Union Bank and was opened in 1895, has filled the space created by the demolition of the cottage. This fine façade has four sixteen feet columns of Aberdeen granite and is surmounted by a figure of Britannia. This frontage in Briggate gives a pleasing aspect to visitors approaching Elland from the north.

Previous page: This aerial view of 1938 clearly shows Elland Bridge and the weir on the extreme left. Kiln End Mills, the National School and St Mary's church are notable landmarks. Close examination reveals many lost yards, passages and ginnels.

From the northern end of the Bridge, looking towards Brighouse, *c.* 1898. This mighty sycamore tree had to be felled to allow the road to be widened near to the bottom of Exley Lane. The entrance to Elland railway station goods yard is to the right with the Station Hotel on the other side of Park Road.

The Power Station, in 1958, has only one cooling tower. Among a forest of mill chimneys the bridge is still clearly seen. Halfway across the bridge is Gasworks Lane, which was the northern exit to Halifax leading up Exley Lane prior to the construction of the Calder and Hebble Navigation. Since 1615 the bridge has been considerably altered and widened on a number of occasions.

ten

Transport

An Act of Parliament of 1757 was passed to allow the building of a canal from Sowerby Bridge to Wakefield by way of Elland. The Calder and Hebble Navigation Company was formed to carry out this work. John Smeaton, the builder of Eddystone Lighthouse, was appointed as engineer. The barge is waiting at the lockkeeper's cottage at Woodside Flour Mill in the 1890s. The coming of the railway in 1839 and the development of the road system and the introduction of petrol-driven vehicles all had an impact on canal traffic. Early in the twentieth century, Robert Carey had a fleet of six barges plying between Sowerby Bridge and Hull.

The patient horse is gradually being overtaken by technology as this scene of the making of part of Huddersfield Road at the Ainleys clearly shows. The traction engine would be able to do the work of many horses.

A national coal strike gripped England in the spring of 1912. Here wagon drivers and a policeman face the camera at Ainley Main with Elland High Banks in the background. The strike was settled a week before Easter.

The Greetland Dying Co. Ltd was a branch of Bradford Dyers Association Ltd (BDA). It had premises between Saddleworth Road and Little Bradley at Greetland. BDA was taken over by Freudenberg, the makers of non-woven fabrics, who in turn were taken over by Sia Fibral, a Swiss company making cleaning materials. This group from the 1920s has John F. Robson of Elland standing in the middle.

The railway line from Manchester to Leeds was opened in 1839 and passed through Elland. Local tradesmen were keen to take advantage of the new transport system and, after a meeting at the Savile Arms, it was decided that Elland justified a station of its own. A station was built and opened in 1842. Two further stations were built near the original site, but each time it was a little further away from the mouth of Elland Tunnel. These stations were opened in 1865 and 1894. The last passenger train, bound for Wakefield, left Elland Station at 9.32 p.m. on 8 September 1962. The freight depot closed in 1965.

The branch line from Greetland (or North Dean) to Halifax was opened in 1844. It was not for a further ten years that Halifax had a through line to Bradford. Here we see Greetland station with Platform 2 on the left. The signal gantry frames the chimney of Lambert's dyeworks in this photograph from 1955.

A locomotive at the level crossing in Green Lane, Greetland, making its way to the Rochdale Road halt and subsequently to North Dean station. The building on the right is Glenholme, for many years a care home for the elderly.

The station at West Vale was near to the top of Green Lane and was on the branch line from North Dean to Stainland and Holywell Green. It was opened on 1 January 1875.

On 14 January 1914, the tramway service was extended from Birchencliffe, Huddersfield to Elland. Before the service arrived it was always intended that the trams should run to West Vale. Here work is underway laying the tramlines in Victoria Road. The shoe shop of Freeman, Hardy and Willis faces into Victoria Road. This new extension to the line was opened on 29 May 1914.

Opposite above: Tram No.63 on route No.7 negotiates the bend at the junction of Jepson Lane and Victoria Road. Bethesda church is on the right. All other visible property in the photograph has since been demolished.

Opposite below: Samuel Roberts set up in business as a coal merchant in 1898 and delivered domestic fuel by horse and cart. He opened an office in Southgate and the supply depot was transferred to Elland station. Samuel Roberts died in 1930. Here two coal wagons and a private car stand at the entrance to Elland station goods yard.

Afterword

Above left: We are indebted to Albert Townsend, who worked as a photographer in Elland in the late Victorian and Edwardian eras. He had a studio at 20 Southgate and later in Victoria Road. An abundance of material he left for future generations to enjoy can be viewed at the rooms of the Greater Elland Historical Society in Northgate, Elland.

Above right: A cabinet print bearing an advertisement for Townsend's photography studio on the back.

Finally, a message to the people of Elland. Persecution Passage in Elizabeth Street is headed by this
peculiar inscription – a carving error or a serious warning?

Other local titles published by Tempus

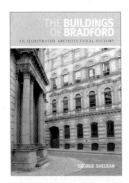

Buildings of Bradford

GEORGE SHEERAN

Bradford has a surprisingly rich building heritage and at a time when the city is undergoing widespread regeneration with buildings of the twentieth century being demolished and earlier, often neglected, buildings restored, this book provides a timely review of significant building survivors and their place in history.

0 7524 3584 1

Brighouse and District

CHRIS HELME

This fascinating collection of over 200 archive photographs illustrates some of the historical developments which have shaped the town of Brighouse. Informative and detailed captions bring additional colour to the images, exploring the buildings, transport and shops of Brighouse and its surrounding settlements, as well as the close-knit communities which have formed the heart of the area.

0 7524 3577 9

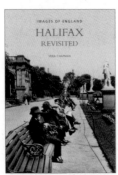

Halifax Revisited

VERA CHAPMAN

This collection of over 200 archive images illustrates the history of Halifax from around the mid-nineteenth century. Characterised by steep slopes and deep valleys, the district has an industrial past of woollen mills powered by water wheels and steam, and of canals and railways. Each image is accompanied by informative captions, providing a lasting record of Halifax as it once was and detailing how the town has developed.

0 7524 3047 5

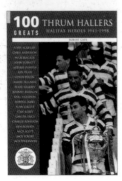

Thrum Hallers: 100 Halifax Heroes 1945-1998

ROBERT GATE

Halifax played their last first-team game at Thrum Hall on 22 March 1998. This book is a tribute to 100 notable Thrum Hallers – all from the post Second World War period – who have left generations of followers with indelible memories of stupendous and grim games, famous victories and infamous defeats.

0 7534 3211 7

If you are interested in purchasing other books published by Tempus, or in case you have difficulty finding any Tempus books in your local bookshop, you can also place orders directly through our website

www.tempus-publishing.com